tourist

poetry
by tak erzinger

Advance Praise for Tourist

'TAK Erzinger's collection *Tourist* acts as a window into a journey through the poet's experiences as well as the locations in the world she has visited in her life. Her poems such as *Chichén Itzá– 1982* and *In Between Days* bring the reader along with her on this journey. It is hard to choose a favourite poem from this collection. As a whole, they offer a panacea to those who've suffered through the past few years of Covid responses.'

— *Amos Grieg, Editor-in-Chief, A New Ulster*

'In her latest poetry collection, *Tourist*, Erzinger masterfully intertwines the beauty and mystery of nature with the joy and suffering of life. With vivid imagery, she holds up a mirror to the moments that defined her and reflects them back like literary snapshots of landscapes and still life paintings. Erzinger reminds us that the past is never far behind, the present is fickle and fleeting, and the future holds the promise of redemption.'

— *Cindy Tovar, founder & editor-in-chief of Hispanecdotes*

'*Tourist* has a beautiful yearning for connection over trauma, the permanent sideshow of the displaced, and, despite it all, transformation and love.'

— *Scott Duncan-Fernandez, Senior editor, Somos en escrito Literary Magazine*

'TAK Erzinger's imagery and metaphor engages us in a world where a woman seeks to understand abandonment, involuntary childlessness, and unconditional love. Readers will enjoy all the stops on this journey that redefine what family could mean. At its heart, *Tourist* reminds us that what we pass on to future generations surpasses blood ties—and when we love freely and deeply, we create family.'

— Liz Whiteacre, author of Hit the Ground and founder of Etchings Press at the University of Indianapolis

'In her collection *Tourist*, TAK Erzinger invites us on a journey. It's a deeply personal one: abandonment, discovery, loss and acceptance vie for space on the page. With the help of winged messengers and flora and fauna that creeps, winds and demands we engage, Erzinger presents otherness and connectedness. She leads us through the flux of the human experience with powerful layers of imagery from the natural world.'

— Madeleine F. White, author of Mother of Floods

Also by TAK Erzinger

At the Foot of the Mountain (Floricanto Press California, 2021)

Stella's Constellation, produced by Alt.Stories and Fake Realities
Podcasts, UK, 2021

Found: Between the Trees (Grey Borders Books Canada, 2019)

"I winked at my own littleness, as people do at their own faults."
–*Jonathan Swift, Gulliver's Travels*

* * *

"We are all visitors to this time, this place.
We are just passing through. Our purpose
here is to observe, to learn, to grow, to love...
and then return home."
–*Australian Aboriginal Proverb*

* * *

For H – thanks for joining me on this journey.

Contents

tourist

Living in a Big Top

I was raised as a spectator. Taught to look with eyes wide open
and a mouth shut closed, a spectre haunting their escapades.

They came in droves in summer. A caravan of exotic animals.
Their foreign tongues licked at my ears and swallowed up my
voice.

They pitched camp in every room, our house became a big top.
Clowns with their magic potions created smoke screens, intoxi-
cating the crowd.

And the performers mastered the tightrope, walking between the
tension points of addiction and their children.

We were the objects that they juggled, like little balls kept in
continuous motion, for entertainment and display. Once the
performance was over, we were tucked away.

Looking back, I can see, the format of these spectacles, the circle
of that stage, developed me into the ringmaster I am today. Away
from the side lines,

at the centre of my life, I know how to interact with its various acts
creating a seamless performance.

I am no longer silent.

Chichén Itzá– 1982

We arrive at the pyramid
over land and sea
in search of something,

hija y madre
with dry mouths
and heavy steps

I interpret language
a child should never hear
read her thoughts, too

a few pesos
for some drinks
does not quench this thirst

our dark faces
scan the mystery
Kukulkán's symbols,

winged serpent
drawn to the sun
like me to her, I think

but what I overlook
she's brought me here
a sacrifice

offering up her guilt
penance for a life
she'd like to leave

and like a snake
she needs to shed it now
pieces fall away

on my lips
skin cracked—assaulted
by what, I cannot say

a silent cry
from a child
she's letting slip away.

Child Interupted

You left me here on a Monday
in September. A heat wave,
cardinals cloaked in sunshine.
In the breeze my hair feathered.
Red-cheeked I wanted to make
for the house, where promises
had slipped from mouth to mouth,
empty as the afternoon sky
your body hovered near mine
stopping short as if repelled.

At school, they asked if you had died,
I recall us standing there between two trees
buried in silence, boughs and branches
reaching out and for a moment I almost
rushed to embrace you; easier to feign
a death than to admit abandonment. I keep
trying to let it go like all those autumn leaves
but the season returns each year, stopping me
in my tracks, the memory so clear I am no longer
blinded by the lie just tormented by the ghosts.

Absconding

Lies cling to your lips
generations of bees under
your tongue. How did you choose
to leave? When did you realise
that you wouldn't return?
I did the dance, I followed
the others

        measured
        convincing.

Honey, in Spanish is
miel

        but it's sweet
        in every culture

it was their stickiness - the children's,
you couldn't endure, leaving you bitter.

When a queen leaves
the hive she abandons
responsibility
lack of direction and hunger left in her wake
but the flowers continue to return
and with no one left to lead
we got lost in the swarm.

Empty

Never left behind in the manner of
a snail shell abandoned at the lip of a garden
lying open, a cavity,   exposed.

Never left behind in the manner of
a plastic bottle adrift, on the hem of a calm, unconcerned sea,
the catch of a starfish to an unknown destination.

Not in this manner.

Left behind
little relics comprised of flesh and bone from a marriage,
a filling that once kept the foundation in place.

Left behind
developing souls, vessels half full, wasted,
as a thirst is quenched elsewhere.

Left behind
Leaving a vacuum, an open wound
children's voices, sound unheard, a gaping hole unable to heal.

Evidence of Survival

Grass sways gently
in the currents, lithe
and golden. In autumn
you slipped away:
indentions left on flesh,
phantom pains, in place of hugs,
maybe we expected this to happen.
The anger, your restlessness
turning up. It's uncertain
how we'll grow, difficult to imagine
the people we'll become. Now that
we've been uprooted, what will be
the best environment? Above the surface,
tender shoots capture precipitation,
suggesting sustainability, evidence
that we have the ability,
to absorb more than we imagined.

In (im)Perfect Agreement

Harmony is what they heard
when he strummed his guitar
my voice connected to his
while he was singing *Margaritaville*,
closing his eyes, garnering attention
I accidentally slipped off key
after, when there was no longer
an audience he yelled at me.
I couldn't keep time, my rhythm
always a little off:
it was my own damn fault.

We would rehearse it all over again,
his talent: a natural performer-
played it all by ear
even though he could never hear me.
Our act had them all fooled
they listened, smiling to themselves
tapping and nodding to the archetypes.
I can still recall those words, they haunt
me like ghosts from random devices:
it could be my fault.

Music and liquor ran through his veins
which may have been why he didn't
find it inappropriate to teach me
those songs, the family protected him
he was their youngest but the performance
had worn thin, away from the stage
the dark nursed his anger and thirst

a song could no longer quench
from behind the curtain the harmony
was lost:
it was never my fault.

The Odyssey of Metamorphosis

Every caterpillar will one day awaken a butterfly
Icarus flying close to the sun
emerging from landlocked confines
defying gravity to escape its maker.

Momentarily, I await quietly camouflaged
and observe a world
unaware of what's to come

Maybe I'll become a creature rooted in the forest
embrace beech with gossamer limbs
and tuck under its loose bark
until I feel safe

When my father's last blow fell
I couldn't bear to wait
I caught a flight across the land
melting all those memories in the sun.

Driftwood

Child, you recall them
your hands in theirs.
You recall, feeling so small

an island between an ocean.
You recall toes in sand, sunshine,
salt and waves of sound –

dialects conjoined. Back then
you could comprehend it all.
Child, like a bright balloon,

high as could be, they pulled
away from you. Your hair,
a knotted net, caught

what was unearthed in the tide.
Child, you recall how they
floated away one by one

after that season by the sea and
it was then, you learned to swim.
Child, you recall wondering

how they could leave,
imprints of touch that
never returned, bruises

covered a waterlogged soul.
You recall a crowded memory,
an empty house void of sound

dust particles navigating
between streams of light,
they told you they'd be there.

You returned time and again
straining to reach for something
to hold on to. You returned on instinct

because it was all you knew.
Adrift, you let the wind
take control, holding fast to the current,

letting the water wash you free.

Fabula: what the stars told

Comet without direction
the universe is boundless
and you're part of it.

You search for a home
racing by it
thinking you're an orphan.

Your wish is to settle
but like any runaway
you're restless.

Cosmic tadpole
sluiced in stars
feeling aimless.

Sun will lead you where
life prospers. Constellations
will map your path.

Remember when the Milky Way
took you in its fold? The smooth
nebula soft against your skin?

We witness you
locked in a galaxy
of regret.

Embrace the liminal space
between the light and dark
surrender.

Discover the key beneath your skin
it opens onto a meadow of cosmos
there, you're housed in heaven.

Find

Unceremoniously, like trees
that rid themselves of leaves
they let her go

she clung hopelessly
their denial, heavy limbs
battered and damaged

exposed to the elements
she drifted from here to there
unable to keep to one place

they had forgotten she was
a cross-pollination of cultures,
theirs, from spine to vein

on the way to the gutter
he caught her
before she could wash away

he knew nothing of her sort
only that she was pleasing
and now she was his

pressed and dried
he kept her
from decomposing

it didn't matter how far
she had fallen, only
that he had found her.

Looking Glass

Instinctively
reaching out
two linden trees,

a reflection
from across the valley
grown faithfully together

how did they get there?
Limbs like tentacles
and lungs exhaling

heavy against the clouds
bellowing in the wind.
Head pressed against

my chest, you breathe
in my fragrance
the potent scent of yeast

flooded by a cascade
of snores. I uprooted
my home

without hesitation,
two trunks
carefully slung in

shoots from a fragile tree.
I arrived, foliage
in full bloom

delicate
but I grew on the spot
with your nourishment

and without
a second thought
you let your toes sink in

waist and chest too
bound to each other
we stand tangled

here
suspended and
surrounded by uncertainty

the sun slicks
so dense with its shine
a mirror

we stare ahead
letting the hill
hold us suspended

much like Rilke,
beauty and terror
happen with each

new season
leaning against the
sky, we keep going

aware that none
of this is final.

Cloudburst

The hopes of lovers build in clouds
then clash as pressure rises
words cause thunderstorms.

Family chatter hangs on wet lips
like the dew across the fields before them
dampens the ground they've covered.

All the emotions ever expressed
spill from heaven, recycled water,
written out in rain.

An empty cradle.

All our emotion-disperse, drift in the sky
clinging to nothing, eventually fall
a sort of heavy serendipitous precipitation.

Promises are clouded by denial
puffs of lies, exhaled
posing as a model couple.

Drizzle is what we hear
our language collected in puddles
drowning out our routine.

Our mouths are open skies
down pouring incomprehensible words
washed away in a sheet of tears.

Foreign

They've sampled my tradition in a spoonful,
too curious to refuse.

I'm a buffet laid out, my language colourful,
a sea teeming with strange delights,

that laps at their ears
the edge of their understanding.

It could be smooth sailing, I've heard,
but I feel a storm in the air

caught between hot and cold, clouded
partitions create boundaries

between concrete and abstract
why must there be one or the other?

I've always been good at balancing
the two from my head to my heart.

They say they care but I can't read
their lips. I beg at their table

like wasps or flies trying to snatch back
pieces they've appropriated, I end up starved.

Low Tide

Ocean
crashes through my blood,
undertow of memories
vein to ventricle,
my tongue reaches
to lick its salt
from my lips,
searching for a taste
that's disappeared.

In solitude
I imagine banquets of sunshine
steaming off our heads,
a liquid sunset
of pink lemonade
bronze hides,
languages duelling
for a dominant spot
on a bed of sand.

From all the places
I've tried to make home,
here I prepare for
a family meal
arroz con pollo,
a table set,
searching for a reflection
on untouched plates
in a sundress with a *mochila*
of a youth that was once me.

Ocean
I try to swim back,
in a diaspora riptide
and start to panic.

From land, you run fingers through wet hair
offering:
"The current has changed,
try treading water and
let nature take its course."

Resident Alien

They'll believe they've tamed her
house broken in a quiet pasture
but never leave a stray alone

she'll discover unexplored
corners to rip apart, open places
long drawn closed and forgotten.

At least, she'll aim to please
memorising every trick, trying
to compensate for misplaced words.

Novelty, it wears off with any pet,
they'll say she's settled now
and won't visit anymore.

Citizen: if you can talk the talk
and walk the walk— you know, *when in...*
But it's still me: from the wild west

heart beating to a different rhythm,
I'm still keeping time
just in another zone.

Dislocated

After I can no longer feel it
they'll ask, how did you get here?

That inquiry about *how* becomes a pain in
itself and I try to put myself back into place

what happens if the injury can no longer set?
Fear returns one moment at a time

as curtains fall open exposing a window
even though my body is here and now

it is fractured by memories, no one can see:
corrupted cells, damaged parts

and whatever could have been
returns not treated or healed

and though I've finally found a place -
to grow whole, questions about

the how I arrived here knock bones
and joints out of place once more

weakening the muscles of my heart.

Nest

Their hands like beaks sift low
lying branches, nimble, limber as reeds.
Raising twigs, they imagine parts
made up of their own, impatient
organs attempting to procreate
any conception
lost in cracked shells
filled with yolk, enough for a meal,
not a lifetime. They hunger through
seasons, their nest emptied of songs
they intended to sing, almost quiet,
nearly gone, they roost anyway
mating for life, contemplating those
embryos, formless drops from the storm.
As the wind whips at the back of their
hollowed out bones, they long for an
unborn promise, made from their love,
washed away in the earth, instead eaten
by worms.

Big Game

Predators
in the city

laid tame by
the country.

Early evening shadows
reveal our stripes

created
by bent blinds.

Every corner of
our corporeal landscape

explored,

left hungry by
childlessness.

Instead we continually
birth our faith,

in love.

Mating season returns-

we're fully aware
roaming two-by-two

we've become
endangered

winter approaches
and we'll become

extinct.

Too beguiled to budge
and find another,

our bodies create
a different beast-

we brave our future
side-by-side

and wallow in our lonely
pride.

Amplexus*

What was it that led them
thus – round mounds of green
like tiny hills, *beasts with
two backs*. I envision them,
smooth bodies slick with wet,
the male clinging to her
smaller frame. Above,
the moon unfurling rivulets of light
their shadows cast along the way,
twines and twangs, huddled in
a soldier's march.

I stop and wonder,
a witness above the pond.
They're gone now, only clouds
of pearls beneath the surface:
life, translucent eggs. We are barren,
no part of us to be left behind –
we hold on to each other anyway,
time against flesh, its universal.
But here, those spawns will emerge
despite remorse or love.

Cyclical. Persistent. We fade away.

Amplexus: the mating embrace of frogs and toads

Too Far Gone

Moth, formed from dust
hovers outside the window
eyelashes fluttering against a lens

out from the thicket
a bit further from the streetlamp
where it's usually drawn

alone, it spies, a translucent
nosey parker,
into a dim lit room

as if a world where landscapes
are created by bodies
membrane of glass, constrains

the moth's journey to here,
an act replayed over and over.
Oscillating its wings against the pane

as the trembling earth silently
witnesses another of its creatures
slowly disappear in the twilight.

Insomnia

I lost it there at the hem of twilight.
It skirted the horizon vanishing in the dark.
Lucidity extinguished at the toll of the last
church bell. It bolted across the field and I
tried to catch it but I couldn't call it back.
Like a deer, it startled away on black coal
hooves. Night confused me and I thought the
mountains wanted to chew me up and spit
me out, I mistook them as teeth.

The moon though, she turned her face
to me and I let myself sink down alone
trying to forget the miles I've covered
reaching for an anchor of light.
What I discovered I cannot say, only
that distance cannot protect me from
that trapdoor that opens to the past.

Craving

Neglect keeps me ravenous with a hallowed out hunger;
Its weight in years is barely manageable. *Haunted – living
memory*. I feed myself with the strangest sustenance.

On good days, I use what I've collected, no thanks to you –
And for a time, I can appreciate what I have become,
full of seasons, ripe and good.

Later, though, we speak again and there I go, bruised
as a windfallen fruit, still lots to offer but overlooked for
circumstances beyond my control. Exposed and tired

I lie there as starvation rises up to meet me again
like a toothless mouth unable to chew, licking
at the only thing you've left me, a lifetime of tears.

The Dead of Night

Awake and outside   among nocturnal animals
something between prey and predator   roaming
below sky   another universe   expanding
a liminal space   without transition
                lost in a quiet riot
the fluid movement of my parts   deft in skill
hunting for peace   caught in a snow globe

by fear   falling past trees   like bodies

or   monsters   encroaching and reaching
restless limbs keep me going   I remember what
keeps me here   insomnia
open windows   pulsing with snores   escaping
maybe   I won't make it back by daybreak
wishes bloom   encouraged by stars
moonlight stains my face   as I fight back sleep
longing for a creature of comfort
                              to sit out the night.

Tethered

Watching the sky open and drool
from my room, exposed to the hills,
I see things that others don't:

the dipper* cutting past, spinning and tumbling
in the swells, the falling star in the dead of night,
a blind mouse lost upon the path.

Like Rhenfield, I want to crawl inside
the stronghold of a straight jacket or cell –
no longer exposed to the blood suckers

who've bled me dry – to finally settle in
these well-worn bones, safely tucked away
from the noise of wagging tongues.

To drift a bit, lay claim to the years
they've stolen from me and hibernate
beneath a blanket of snow. Committed:

tethered here, I can no longer roam,
nor be touched. I'll take this damp soil and
when no one's looking, bury my shame.

*the white-throated dipper, water fowl

Awake in the Sky

I realised the sky
recognised me, she
wrapped her cool blanket around
my body, its surface full of stars and moths
I could see as never before, Orion
almost tickling my cheeks,
only a few clouds between me
and another universe or time
silhouettes of trees full and breathing
witness to an otherwise still night
I couldn't sleep within
the small hours, instead I floated
in that liminal space
a guest, somewhere between
life and death
but not in a dream
finding quiet and comfort
in the order of things beyond.

Feral

Often when I awake, surrounded by purrs and fur,
their bodies wrapped around my torso,
their eyes as green as mine – I believe I am one of them.

I believe I can steal through the field and sit
beside a mouse hole until flesh is caught between
my claws. And the creatures big and small,

I hear them rumbling in the belly of the forest
they lead me to the corridor of a secret place,
tracking what others cannot see.

And my eyes they flare in the pitch of night and laps
they become free game and beds, they are all the same.
But it's when I slink down alone beyond the path without

a care, no haunting memories or remorse, past the taunting
creek, through the black matted trees, I can finally
ignore the calls that are supposed to lead me home.

Tattooed on this Landscape

Sky has peeled opened above the far-off mountains
and at my feet wind whips, climbing up the hills.

On this day, snowdrops have emerged
surrounding a lonely stump

like with many amputees the pain
still comes and goes.

Even so, here roots are still trying to take hold.
Severed from you at a tender age

life sprouted from a half-formed place

now aged

upon this landscape my ruined cells
are pained by winter's chill

laced with your blood and trauma
my molecules will leave stains—inconsequential ash

and this sadness too will eventually fade.

Love in the Time of Quarantine

Hills
heave euphoric
bruised in crocuses

Overwrought
heaven ruptures
in rain

Spring appears
sheathed
in uncertainty

Sweating
out the cold
fevered by wind

Next to me
your mouth open
a hive

Sweet
humming in
familiar warmth

Exhaling
relief and comfort
a ritual aubade.

Waiting to be Delivered

Boxed up like parcels
folded in on ourselves

cordoned off in rooms
we wait to be delivered

remainders of unused things
tucked away from hungry hands

but spring cannot be boxed in
a bragging sky

robin's egg blue
meadows coughing up flowers

as we rattle in these confinements
our bones lie dormant

like tulip bulbs
packed up last season

waiting for the sun
to pull us from this buried place

dispatching us into a changed world.

Foxes

What if I can't be kind enough?
What if I'm unable to repent?
The beast in me, wild, instinctual,
takes what it needs.
If I can share these desires,
would it feel safer for you?
Even as humans hold the world hostage,
the moon still waxes at night
gauzy light spreads across the land,
illuminating hills and rustling trees,
spilling onto lakes and mountains
floating on the sea,
while the vixen calls for her mate
you remain steadfast offering yourself
over and over no matter the risk.
Even as foxes hunt low against the grass
we avoid becoming each other's prey
we fight to survive exposing our fears
struggling with our baser instincts
as the worlds seems to close
in around us.

Inside Out

The storm enabled the sky
to express itself as needed

drove us inside
like snails or turtles

and we huddled against walls
thinking we were safe there

dreaming about flying
the adventures we once had.

Thunder interrupted our
thoughts - loud and imposing

its weight of clouds
its mouth of rain,

more emotional than any
thing we dared to show.

We listened carefully like
friends interpreting its woes,

silently. Then the sun, a
gentle hand, dried away

the wet and for a moment
even though we had been

spared, we mourned all
that had been washed away

even the people and places
we had never met, would never go.

Vacancy

Betrayed in a borrowed house
she said, "I've lost my mind."

She drifts into song
lyrics echo from childhood

she holds still, in a room, calling
for sisters long gone

nameless strangers, children, visit
sometimes taking her hand

there's a hole in her memory
and a void in her eyes.

She wants someone to take her home
but her memory is unforgiving.

Youth arrives, an attendant, bringing
sunshine, fresh cut grass and summer

first love returns in a dream, not the
young man who pushes her through the garden

and her nurse hums, "Sail away ladies"

as her life blurs
against the window pane.

Optical Illusion

Disappearing   behind the window:
universe in four walls,
spotlight, a bulb on a cord,
moth wings swishing like skirts
and ruffled, a well-worn costume.
Between acts: night and day –
Everything is smokescreens and mirrors.
Wanted: an audience   people
around the stage with its tricks,
a crowd,   front and centre.
Next month perhaps.

Every week is a season. Summer was long with drought,
nearly no fall at all: winter assaulted,
and again, we've been driven inside.
Memory might fade, but that's what photos remind us of,
imbued with images and a life once lived,
captured in a small space.

Return: el Día de los Muertos

They return as
moths. Impervious

to the artificial
landscape between

the hills. Ancestors
soft-winged, snug

against the round
bellied sky, led by

a heavy moon.
Stars, reflected

blades of grass
crowned by dew.

Maybe it's been years
but history flows

here and is free.

Centuries later,
I'm living proof

relic of blood and bile
where east goes south

European bones
encased in native tissue

just like moss grown
on a tree, in harmony.

Pale ghosts flutter
against the screen

seeing the peace
bred in me

black, brown and white
housed in one place

haunted by the past
a lineage of rope, fire and water.

Heartburn

Yesterday I discovered what anaemia is:
quiet snowflakes turned the sky pale,
the grass capped in frost or is it called *escaracha?*
I whisper the word and try to hold on to it,
the way my tongue pushes against my teeth.
The day my mother departed,
cold moved in and innocence was frozen,
along with my meaning of all those words:

mami,   madré.   hija,   niña

tongue-tied something got lost in translation.
They've given me iron to strengthen me,
if only it could forge us back together.
I try to eat my way back to you, so much flesh and blood.
I try to recover every dish you ever made me but I'm
still hungry, surrounded by empty plates
and the aroma of what was served.
Waves of indigestion chase me out of a dream.

Heirloom

It sits a little tight on my wrist,
a golden band beneath emerald hills.
Perennial, green buds, the Muzo valley*
glistening in a tropical shower.
It was hers but it hung looser then,
like a handcuff, now it's mine.
If I sold it or it was stolen
I might be able to forget her accent as
it escaped from an open door or
her dark skin, like café con leche, foreign.
She has kept her distance though,
the bracelet a yoke fastening us together.
Our blood not strong enough to keep us working.
Her burden heavy as if a stone,
if only I could skip it on the water,
letting it sink, disappearing out of sight.

*valley in Colombia where emeralds are mined.

Blood Gold

My mother had a coffer of gold
and two languages
every holiday she gave
me a piece of jewellery, the
weight heavier and heavier
as she unloaded the responsibility
now I wear it like a leaden anchor
dug into the land of Colombia –
a noose of memories
attached to the walls of
a colonial house, dangling from guava trees
coming in waves like that of the Atlantic
full of phantoms: Afro, Indigenous, and Spanish.

I fiddle with the contours of the chains
searching for how she could let it all go?
Pieces hanging on to me
links to something done unseen
and think if she can give it up, so can I.
I think emancipation.

I ask the pawn shop,
'How much is it worth?'
I'm told a ton and I look
in the mirror, the heirlooms
clinging around my skin
I see the beauty my mother
refuses to see, I feel the pain
of it too. It's hard to bear the weight
of who you are and where you

come from, how easy it is
to get lost in translation.
I choose to uphold her legacy
no matter the cost.

Margarita

I imbibe you, memories blur
and I become drunk.
It's dizzying to go to that place –
I reach for another,
hoping to conjure back that feeling.
The taste becomes too much though,
and the initial sweet sip turns bitter.
Fluid
you pass right through me:
sangre de mi alma – una familia dañada–
I was too young and tender to understand
what adults could do, I needed to fill
the vacuum and you offered confidence.
I didn't realise it wouldn't last a lifetime.
Ripened things turn overnight
and I tried so hard to not get bruised.
I'm not good at swallowing spoilt things,
I've tasted too much rotten love.
You forced me to come clean though,
cold turkey, but it doesn't mean
I don't miss you.
Every time a milestone arrives
I try to serve up what I've learnt but
end up swilling salt from fallen tears.
Sometimes I savour those
moments in mouthfuls
even if the hangover still causes
me too much pain.

Fruta

The harvest my mother refuses to see,
the promise that hangs about my trunk
from brown, well-worn branches,
I deliver it to each reunion

every time fuller, riper and blooming with life
like the mango trees lining that familiar street
supple, yet as graceful as the egret that flies
above them cutting through the night sky.

Two years on, she sold *el piso*,* the place
where I planted hope along the intercoastal,
whispered inner secrets and thrived,
there Abuela loved me anyway and because.

From her little room, she watched this
hybrid grow, roots shooting out wildly
with no where to anchor them. She could
see the soil wasn't quite right, she tended to

me anyway. You have no memory of how green
I was or the sunlight I was searching for, you
left me in the shade. Like her, you were silent,

but unlike you, she knew the value of this
strange fruit and its need to be preserved.

apartment

Bellyfull

Inside my belly, I carry fire
diluted dreams of my ancestors.

Though their lives have passed
insatiable hunger remains

like an eager tree in spring
I am fruited with their legacy.

Even as I have ripened
they refuse to drop away

I let their lineage emerge
I will not fight against them

but turn to what feels instinctual
I will use their leftovers, partake in

recipes like theirs but not without
my own touch, inside my own vessel

letting fresh ingredients – fecund
and raw wholly blend and boil.

Honouring that half a world and
half a century ago flames flickered

and bare bodies cooked
seasoning the taste to come.

Forecast

—after Polite Safety Notice by Mark Riddes
Out there, everywhere a woman past her prime
is rolling through the streets, low rumbling thunder.
Closer than you think women, are gathering clouds.
I know you must have heard of it.
They open their mouths, round eyes of storms.
Beware and adapt. Like hurricanes, moist air
rising, opposing forces have whipped them up.
Their season has arrived.

A force of nature. Unstoppable. You cannot escape it.

Out there, everywhere, a little girl is standing up in class,
saying what should have been said a long time ago.
Her words swarms of bees unable to be contained
absconding through the halls and windows
creating an impenetrable buzz. Be in awe,
she has learnt by watching all the adults' mistakes,
a film on repeat, stuck in that same scene,
over and over again. The others will follow her flight.
Once captured, it escapes out of every pore like sweat inevitable
in heat.

A force of nature. Unstoppable. You cannot escape it.

Out there, everywhere, young women are starting families,
still pressured to perform following the pack,
zooming and nooming, contained in little squares,
they'll share every moment in an instant.

Others, barren in the race, barricaded
by careers, hiding from the clocks that keep turning over on
dainty phone wrist watches.

But out there, the weather is changing. Throw open the doors.
The landscape created long ago, needs reshaping.
Together it can be tended and nurtured.
Like stars, or slow growing trees the end will not be seen
by this generation but its growth can sustain the future.

A force of nature. Unstoppable. You cannot escape it.

Seeds (women sow)

Seeds scattered from afar
have come to life
nodding in the wind

divided by colours but
not in their spirit
to thrive.

Heat
a reminder
of seasons past

and decaying
blooms long faded
not forgotten.

Summer
the strong whiff of earth
treaded on by ripened girls

is not kind to all
it scorches those
without shelter

and as it exits
the roll of thunder
loud and impending arises

a cacophony of voices
from every corner
of the landscape.

I observe
from the hilltop
as dozens

of wildflowers
shake their heads
in fury and defiance

taking up the battle
of storms that rage
time and time again.

Abscission

Alight, I let myself go like
the leaves of our ginkgo tree

I can no longer hang on
to the season before

although its stories will
remain dormant in my limbs.

Rings around my trunk
that no one will see

like stretch marks or cellulite
I keep them buried

under layers. Here
before autumn succumbs

to winter I thirst for
the last drops of sunshine

lean into its warmth
lingering like a tourist

whose holiday is ending
I wonder if I'll have

a second spring as
silver threads spread

across my head. I feel
empowered by the climate

but let down by the
environment

unsure about
what I'll leave behind.

It's funny how when
I'm finally naked, exposed

I'm the most invisible
I hope I can continue

to grow, knowing
I'm the last of this line.

Mid-life

Under my coat, I pulsate
like a Dutch bulb ready to
emerge from its sepal.
I've already faced the darkest day
and settled in this soil
I want to rush this moment,
to reveal what I have become
but the travel has been more robust
than I've anticipated
I need to wait out this hibernation.
Half a life away now, a lingering
fog begins to lift, I notice even the
meagre trees are full of buds,
I think I hear a birdsong.
Let the days slowly lengthen; I
might not catch its first light but
my thoughts turn towards its warmth.
In spring, I shall emerge shawled
in ripened skin, perennial and strengthened.
Far off, a young girl departs from home
bearing down the path,
her beacon, the promise of the journey.

In Between Days

Often, I pass that little girl on the street
she whispers: see me.
Eyes full like the sky and moon,
her lips hold a secret
but her face speaks
a wide constellation of freckles
her body seems to float
unaware, she balances the world
at her feet.
I recognise her curiosity and catch
a whiff of her innocence.
Between the public garden
and the cemetery we pass each other
I could pretend not to see her
and then she startles me and
says "hello" –
my whole life rushes by
in the afternoon light
I lose her as she slips round the corner
and just like the sunshine that warms
my cheeks youth returns for an instant
and I am reminded how I ended up here.

Lenguaje Resonante | Echoing Language

Yo hablo, yo hablo así, yo hablo así, en mi corozón...
When I began to speak, I parroted
Mariposas instead of *butterflies*
and they appeared to be tropical
but I realised I was landlocked and
it was winter with dusty snowflakes
taking over from an unknown place
but in me it was hot, *patacone* crumbs
clung to my salted lips and a sunspot
in a photo held me closer to her
but language and places have changed
days so faraway from palm trees and
Caribbean waves recede with miles
and miles of exile, my empty mouth
open and trembling a ghost of words
veiling a forgotten culture
everywhere colours I can no longer
describe, it's all bled together now
into a spring day— migrating
I've returned, listening at night
feeling my turning tongue inside me
I awaken that vernacular through
song and sound again and again before
I sleep and from abroad I stitch memories
and echo words under my skin
slowly misplaced phrases return
softly revealing their delicate wings.

Waterway

Follow me, it directed
the way a calf is steered by its mother.
Docile and curious, I obey
hugging the water's edge.

The creek was made redundant
by the old factory but has not retired.
Repurposed by stones and roots

flowing for treading fish
and the trill and song of birds,
it sustains natural life

no longer concerned with
a waterwheel or profit
I watch it, as it

runs and leads
and laugh,
because I cannot keep up.

Diplomats

Diplomats negotiating
like blood brothers
we've bled for each other

as a couple,
sometimes we get
lost in translation.

Outside
the landscape rolls out
before us

we speak to the land
and the land speaks to us
multilingual

we listen
realising we're just travellers
passing through

collecting experiences
strangers facing each other,
are we not the same?

A lifetime
we've questioned
our place

through dirt, rock and water
together we discover
there are no boundaries.

Time Machine

Spying an aeroplane smooth and silver
far above land, between space and rock,
living two lives:

above sea-level, afraid of heights
saddled by a dialect, my tongue
blooms with foreign wounds,

I long to return to the shallows of the sea –
floating – or taste the crust of an *arepa*,
salted like your skin. Touch down

on a landing strip and stake claim
to abandoned places with starfruit trees
shining ripe, straining to be plucked.

Let's return: we'll tread the wide, once
teeming asphalt, still hot from the sun.
Jet-lagged, no one will notice how much

we've changed.

Tumour

Inside your head
waves roar like
in a shell: cochlea.

An island's formed there
and I long to rescue you
from that place

nestled between
sound and thoughts,
I worry you're drowning

and what about if you
no longer hear my voice?
Then we'll speak eye to eye

and you will always
understand the
rhythm of my heart

later when it's time
to cede that site
we'll create a language

all our own—
our love
with our whole voices

will grow in unspeakable tenderness.

Precious Scars

Out by the sea
I'm trying to recover those
small pieces of our relationship.

I can't figure out,
how and what fits back together
I cut myself like on sea glass.

My confusion lies
between what was said
and what we feel,

wide as the divide between
our lips and heart.
Yet our history of love

should be enough for always.
I made my heart your heart
but neither of us can breathe

and as we sit on the beach
trying to create something new
things still don't fit as before

a ritual and a sacrifice,
I give you my offering,
a repair –

What do the Japanese call it,
Kintsugi?

You accept it as if we were always that way.

Between the Sun and the Moon

Together
we are the sea
separately
billions of drops
deep enough
to hold many lives
our voices waves,
loud enough
to drown out the storm
strangers like us
of salt and water
together
we are one
tides that ebb and flow
raging against the shore
reshaping
the landscape
every day.

Mundo

The place where the mountains kiss the sky
the canvas that catches the light and the palette
from where nature comes alive
a schedule measured in seasons – weather,
journey through storms
blinding fog
cacophony of crickets
armfuls of sunlight
comfort beneath trees
solitude broken by chattering leaves
wildlife hidden in plain sight
with sounds unseen
wind carried in, Sahara sand
droplets delivered in parcels of clouds
exhaled from dolphins and whales.
A lifetime of migration
like that of birds or snowflakes
individual routes from cities across lands.
Einheimisch or native,
I think, what does that mean?
Then it rolls quietly off my tongue: *mundo*.
All I see, is the place where the mountains kiss sky,
boundless, untethered, unconcerned
about whether we belong   or not.

Lingua Franca

The season was warm, the hills abundant in colour.
The forest at the end of the path opened its mouth wide.
Right away I understood the trees,
they spoke of sanctuary.
Finally, I could comprehend the direction the *kites**
were pointing me in, the meaning of their whistles
and the quiet conversation between the woods and the wind
and the reaction of the brook,
its laughter welling up at my feet
drawing up to me today and everyday
and the midday sun thick on branches
molasses, heavy and golden
spilled over the *dipper** dancing to the chatter
upon a bald stone and then,
tumbling into the small shoals
systematic and quick by design.
Butterflies gossiped among the first flowers
of the season, straining to hear over the bees' humming,
what's new, and the outline of mountains written in stone
whispered quietly, stoic but approvingly—
the day abandoned to the weather's mood, and
the landscape textbook, its vocabulary ringing
in my ears communicating as clear as the sky above
and the blue tit skipping beside me, along the shrubs,
every syllable, every sound, was understood here,
a lingua franca or universal tongue, an overture
to a way of life that is often forgotten.

**Kites, Dipper: a type of hawk & waterfowl*

High Time

There are things
that are taken for granted,
the stealth of growth:
eager buds crowning
through dirt and snow
reaching for life or a family home
it's believed to be a given—
a place between two pillars
supported by a solid foundation
a spot where you should have thrived,
instead left in a pile like an abandoned harvest.

Let us rise above it! Look to each other
found friends, our call to the outside
the muffled cry of the wild
drumming in our ears.
Until the next day breaks
reminding us, where home is:
together facing towards the sun.

Sanctuary

When sadness swells in me
I turn to the path, the one less travelled,
I listen to my feet beat against the ground below me
keeping time with my heart
and at the water's edge I catch the heron's joy,
it's contagious
I arrive at peace between the trees
as they rise to meet the sun
unconcerned by the worries of the world
for a moment I am a conduit of wild things
unencumbered
I exist under a naked sky
just another creature in the woods
free, I can finally rest for a moment.

Tourist

What this journey through time and space isn't,
a fissure split between earth and spirit or a
mere yawn of seasons, but maybe it's the ignorance
about the end, its invisible grasp that holds us
in a headlock we'll never be able to escape from
that steers us free.

Our bodies a compass being navigated
led like sailors by the stars or bees by flowers.
Every day the sun, yellow orange yellow, hope
pulling life up and out with its invisible force.
Travelers   we are seeds blown asunder by chance
some settled close to their origins

others adrift over land and sea, no matter
all of us just passing through, witnesses or tourists
to a time and place, waves rolling in and moving out
forgetting that we're all headed towards the same destination
and just like birds in migration our souls will know
where to go, leading towards the final excursion.

Our shells, souvenirs left upon the shore.

Acknowledgements

Many heartfelt thanks to the editors of the following magazines, journals and reviews, in which some of the poems have previously appeared.

Agape Review poem "Sanctuary"

Anthropocene Poetry Journal poem "Heirloom"

Anti-Heroine Chic, v. 17 poem "Empty"

The Be Zine poems "Amplexus" "Evidence of Survival"
"Big Game"

The Cajun Mutt Press poem "Return: El Día de los Muertos"

Chiricú Journal, University of Indiana poems
"Chichén Itzá– 1982"
"Blood Gold"

Celestal Review poems "Cloudburst"
"The Odyssey of Metamorphosis"

Confetti poem "Craving"

Crowstep Journal poem "Lenguaje Resonante"

Culture Cult poem "Lenguaje Resonante" 2nd edition
Dashboard Horus poem "Resident Alien"

Festival for Poetry poem "Love in the Time of Quarantine"

Gertrude's Writing Room poems "Foxes" "Inside Out" "Mundo"

Hispanecdotes Journal poems "Fruta" "Margarita"

Kitchentable Quarterly poem "Driftwood" 1st edition

Lothlorien Poetry Journal poems, "Mid-life"
"In (im)Perfect Agreement"
"In Between Days"
"Waterway"

LoveLove Magazine poems "Inside Out" "Driftwood"
2nd edition

45 Magazine poem "Nest"

Mockingowlroost poems "The Dead of Night"
"Time Machine"

Mono. Journal poem "Sopita"

The Muse poem "Waiting to be McMaster University Delivered"

Open Skies Anthology poem "Mid-life"

The Opiate poems "Absconding" "Forecast"

Otherwise Engaged Literary Arts poem "Mundo" 2nd edition

Pear Tree – The Literary Hatchet poems "Diplomats"
"Lingua Franca"

The Rational Creature
New York University poem "Optical Illusion"

The Raven's Perch poems "Tumour" "Dislocated"
"High Time"

Red Penguin Press poems "Seeds (women sow)"
Bloom edition "Evidence of Survival"

Reedy Branch Review poem "In Between
Pitt Community College "Days"

The Spire of Light Journal poem "Abscission"
Andrew University

Toho Journal poem "Heartburn"

Vita Brevis Press poem "Too Far Gone"

The Voices Project poem "Fabula: What the stars told"

Welter Baltimore University poem "Vacancy"

Whimperbang poem "Low Tide"

Write On! Pen to Print poem "Bellyful"

About the Author

TAK Erzinger is an award-winning poet. Her collection *At the Foot of the Mountain* (Floricanto Press California, 2021) won the University of Indianapolis Etching Press, Whirling Prize 2021 for best nature poetry book. It was also a finalist at The International Book Awards 2022, Willow Run Book Awards and Eyelands Book Awards. Her first audio drama *Stella's Constellation* was produced by Alt.Stories and Fake Realities Podcasts, out of the UK. She is an American/Swiss poet and artist with a Colombian background. She lives on a foothill of a Swiss alp with her husband and cats.

About the Press

Sea Crow Press is committed to amplifying voices that might otherwise go unheard. In a rapidly changing world, we believe the small press plays an essential part in contemporary arts as a community forum, a cultural reservoir, and an agent of change. We are international with a focus on our New England roots.

Sea Crow Press is named for a flock of five talkative crows you can find anywhere on the beach between Scudder Lane and Bone Hill Road in Barnstable Village on Cape Cod.

According to Norse legend, one-eyed Odin sent two crows out into the world so they could return and tell him its stories. If you sit and listen to the sea crows in Barnstable as they fly and roost and chatter, it's an easy legend to believe.